67

Ontological

Studies

Sixty-Seven Ontological Studies

49 Poems & 18 Photographs

Jan Zwicky & Robert V. Moody

FREEHAND BOOKS

An earlier version of this book was published as a limited edition in 2020 by Barbarian Press under the title *Fifty-Six Ontological Studies.*

Freehand Books acknowledges the financial support for its publishing program provided by the Canada Council for the Arts and the Alberta Media Fund, and by the Government of Canada through the Canada Book Fund.

FREEHAND BOOKS
515 – 815 First Street SW
Calgary, Alberta T2P 1N3
www.freehand-books.com

Book orders:

UTP Distribution
5201 Dufferin Street
Toronto, Ontario M3H 5T8
Telephone: 1-800-565-9523
Fax: 1-800-221-9985
utpbooks@utpress.utoronto.ca
utpdistribution.com

Library & Archives Canada Cataloguing in Publication Data:

Title: Sixty-seven ontological studies : 49 poems & 18 photographs / Jan Zwicky & Robert V. Moody.

Names: Zwicky, Jan, 1955– author. | Moody, R.V., 1941– photographer.

Identifiers: Canadiana 20220229740 | ISBN 9781990601095 (softcover)

Classification: LCC PS8599.W53 S59 2022 | DDC C811/.54—dc23

Canada Council for the Arts / Conseil des Arts du Canada
Alberta
Canada

Contents

9 Armchair
10 Moon
11 New Year
12 *Table, Chair, Bed*
13 Library
14 Despair
15 Cold
16 Beached Seal, Dying
17 *Strait of Juan de Fuca*
18 Love
19 Snow
20 *Clearing Storm*
21 Lupercal
22 Skin
23 February
24 Now
25 *Driftwood*
26 March, Olympic Peninsula
27 Equinox
28 Effervescence
29 *Sakura*
30 Skylight
31 *Lightfall*
32 *Ice Lake*
33 Spring Walk
34 May
35 Sex
36 *Independence*
37 Spring in the Mountains
38 *Bookseller*
39 Old Books
40 Old Blues
41 The Great Composers
42 At the Jewish Memorial in Prague
43 *Water Mirror Garden*

44 Standing in line at the bank after reading lines by Roo Borson
45 *Calla Lilies*
46 After Flight
47 Night Air
48 Sunshine
49 Light Industrial Park
50 *Dominion Telegraph*
51 Befriending Wind
52 *Our Lady Queen of Angels, La Placita*
53 Crying
54 Late Style
55 Drought
56 Feet
57 Lullaby
58 Lavender
59 String Quartet
60 Badlands
61 *Cottonwood*
62 Rocky Shore
63 Harvest
64 *Snow Geese*
65 Earth Season
66 Ars Poetica
67 *Lingering Garden*
68 Autumn
69 *Scholar's Study*
70 Translation
71 View from the Ferry
72 Up at four a.m.
73 Waking
74 *Chair*
75 Winter

77 Acknowledgments
78 *Photograph Locations*

67

Ontological Studies

Armchair

Do you remember, my friend, the doorway
we had to widen for your bulk?
And that pole lamp with the broken brass ferrule —
the nights we three saw dawn together!

Guardian of lost paperclips and half-glimpsed visions,
you, who were old, and warm, and strong.
You, who embraced me like the earth,
while my mind went, alight, among the houses of the dead.

Moon

Moon, there you are again,
solo in the pale blue sky.
I agree it's strange,
the way I stare.
The snow on the mountains
is as white, their dark rock
as remote. I, too,
said goodbye to the earth
long ago.
                    But, you see,
I touch it still.
With my hands, my feet. My eyes.

New Year

Brilliant sun, the wind
high in the canopy.
Out by the road,
the tangle of alders is a cliff
in the low southwest light:
their white trunks, and the ice
in their cinnabar branches:
it flashes and gleams.

Like forgiveness when we fail.
And forgiveness when we fail again.

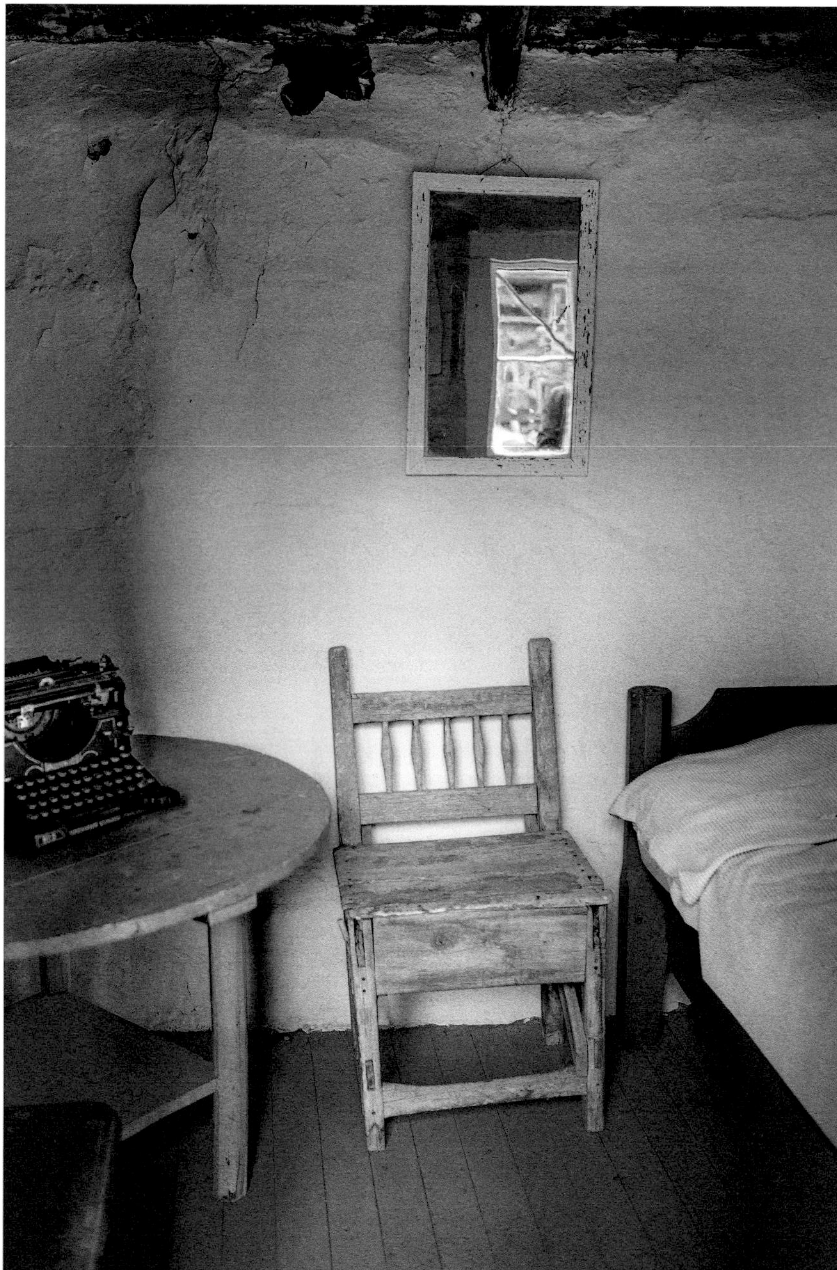

Library

Enter. The calm ranks stretch
before you, dank, faintly stuffy,
a cosmos of introverts:
ten thousand, ten thousand thousand
voices, and not one
glad hand. Ah, books,
your silence! — Like old snow,
deep, without a footprint,
even in the heat of June.

Despair

The fine grey snow of first light.
Look: the holes

you've pickaxed in your sleep
thinking, thinking.

Did they lie to you? Run.
Maybe the ferry is still waiting.

There's the old ache in the shoulders,
but some fates remain shapeless.

Empty your pockets.
They are sewn shut.

Cold

It comes to the door,
it comes to the window,
it enters in silence
and doesn't take off its hat.

Outside, where it walked,
the leaves lie edged
with frost. And you

are the only thing
that moves. Resistless.
The loose ends of the earth
tucked in.

Beached Seal, Dying

It could be
I shouldn't wait with you.
When I'm dying
I might want to be alone, without
distraction, work to do
unhooking and unbraiding,
loosening the seams. I'll be glad

if it's like this, though,
under open sky, near dusk,
the bow wave of the distant ferry
motionless, a gull
tipped sideways for a second
in the wind.

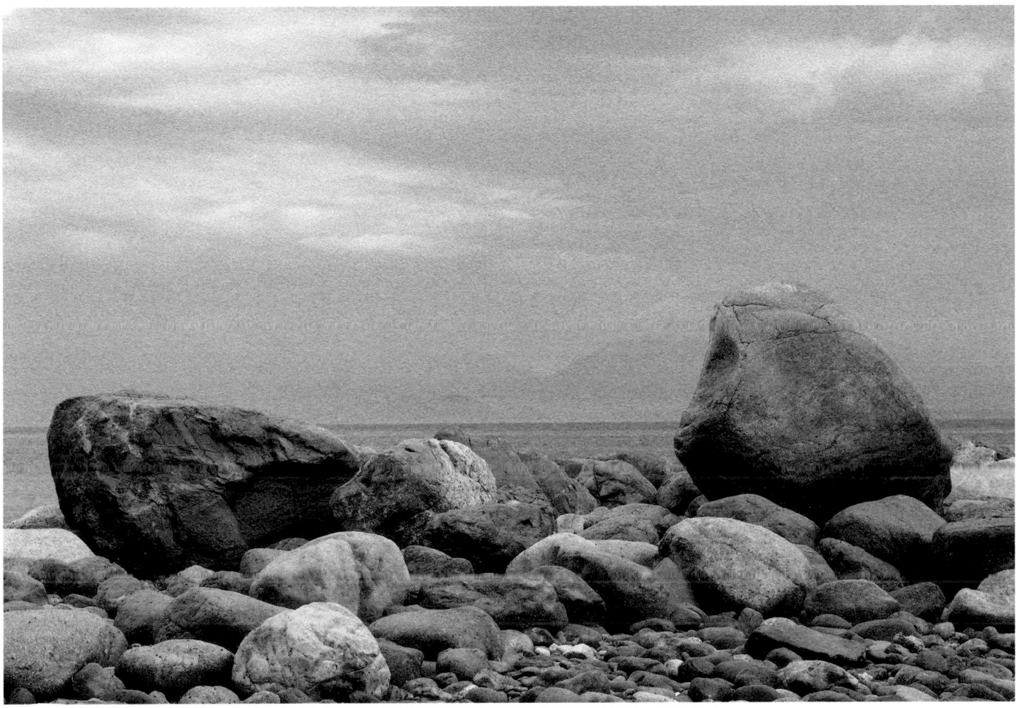

Love

In the winter city,
when I must walk the winter streets,
it is a shawl, the finest, toughest, warmest
wool. When I'm in the subway malls,
it's space, a cordoned breath,
between me and the blare. But here,
I don't need memory, your arms
are muscle, blood and bone.
And I drink from the spring.

Snow

In the night, the eyes
no longer see. In snow,
we find our way
by sight alone. It falls
unthinking, fills
the heavy afternoon
with white.
And you should sleep now,
let snow fill you
as it fills the world.
Soundless its erasure.
Gone the coloured clutter
of your loves.

Lupercal

At last, faint light into the evening,
buds like felted seed pearls
on the cherry tree.
More jars empty in the pantry
than are full, and one last squash
poised, dusky, on the cutting board.
The bleak magnificence of spring
just out of sight. Flame
rushing through life's vacant core.

Skin

The shine, like an old suit,
where you're taut across
the bone. The seams
where you've been mended,
not invisibly.
Why can't I forgive you
that you've grown old? You are
what holds me in,
what lets me, makes me,
be alone.

February

The sharp shadow of the eave on the porch,
fir needles dry the far side of it,
frozen in a skim of ice on this.

Hello, spider. Hello, old broom.
Hello, world, you who also know
nothing you can say.

Now

You are not your own.
In you, through you,
what lives itself.
No stopping it,
no making it

go away. Everybody
feels it: the old
pine, the new
pine beetle, the fire,
the old wind,

the new grass.

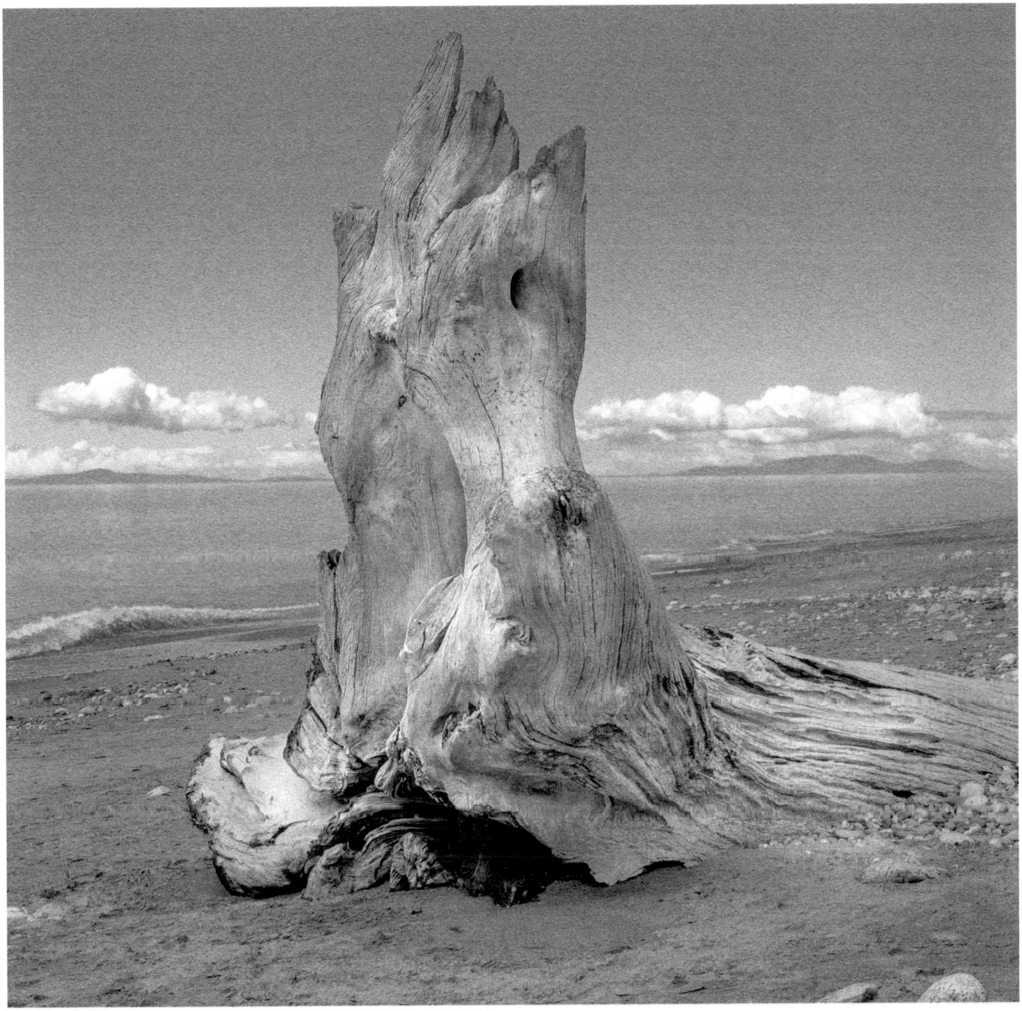

March, Olympic Peninsula

Heavy snow, the dark trees
silent in their cloak of inwardness.

Too late: we lift our hands to shade our eyes
from sun, the evenings lengthen,

and we turn our faces outward
to the world. The stillness

that we leave behind unthought
and then undone.

Equinox

For now night falls
deliciously, and moonlight
through the alders, hung with catkins,
and the plum tree's ghost above the pond.
The saw-whet owl,
and silence, then
the frogs once more. And maple tips
that swell into the dark, the sword grass
lifting, all night things
called up and out into the stars.
Their stillness, flung and reaching.
Wave on wave,
the slow turn of that glittering
to dawn.

Effervescence

The wine opens its arms
and its soul streams upwards,
breaking back into the air.

The long throat of being,
its liquid body.

And the soul — is it
breath, or light?

Sparkling, we say,
the radiance of dissolution
bursting on our lips.

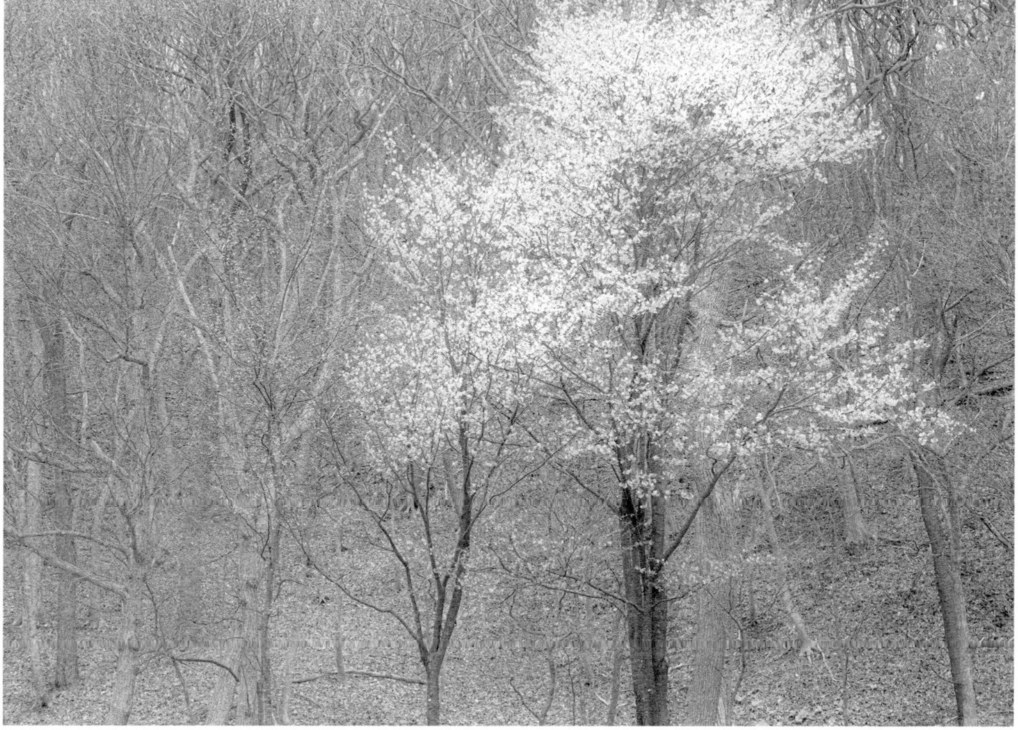

Skylight

A bowl of stones floats
on its table in the milky light.
New light, washed and springy
like a still-damp fleece.
Look up: the clouds there,
framed by the edges of the opening.
Defined this way, you see them
clearly: the patterns, the complexity.
It pierces you somehow; you think
it is more beautiful
even than the sky.

And what you feel
is right, though what you think
is not. Your sadness
is the sadness of a thing that almost
can remember how it was
to walk upon the ground.

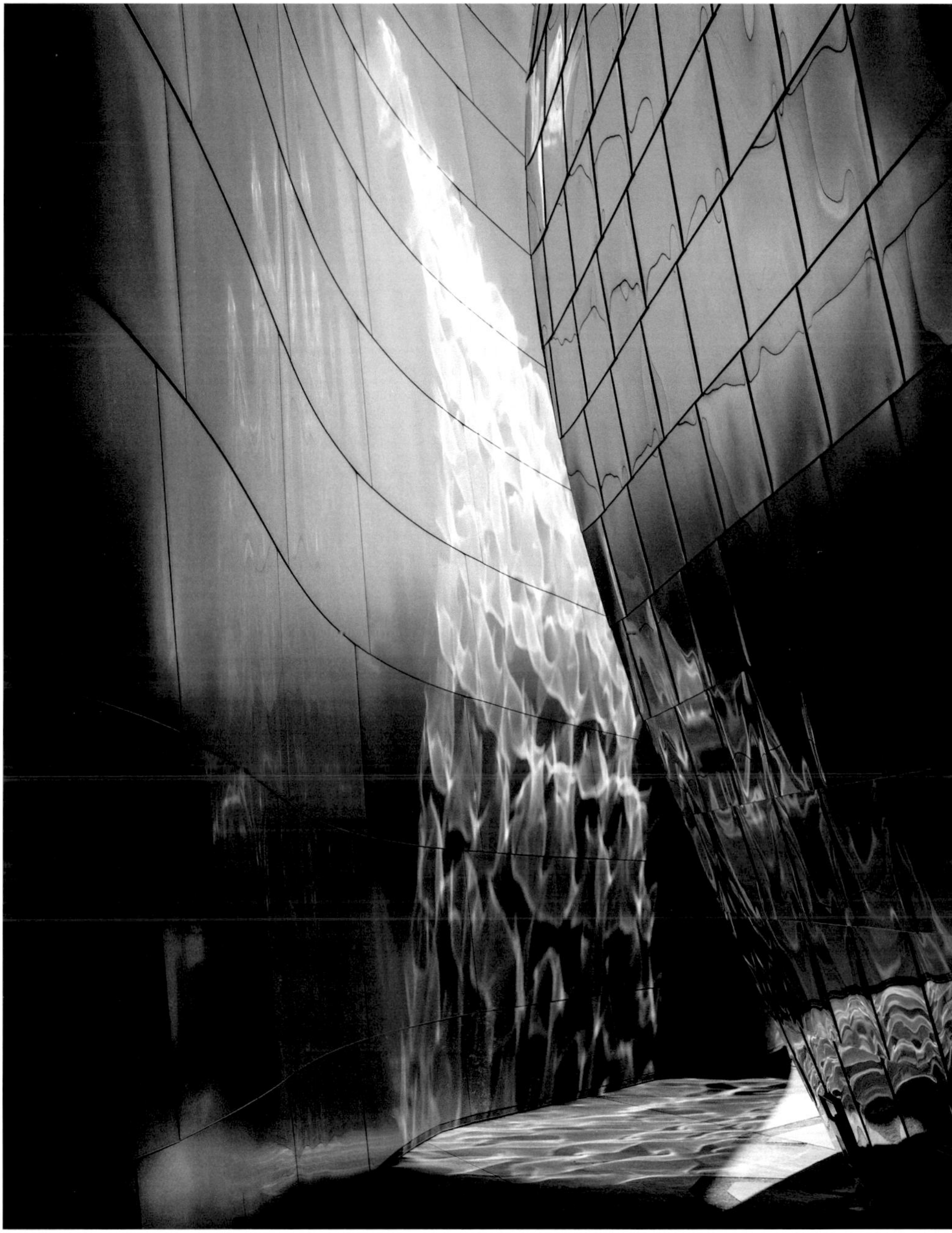

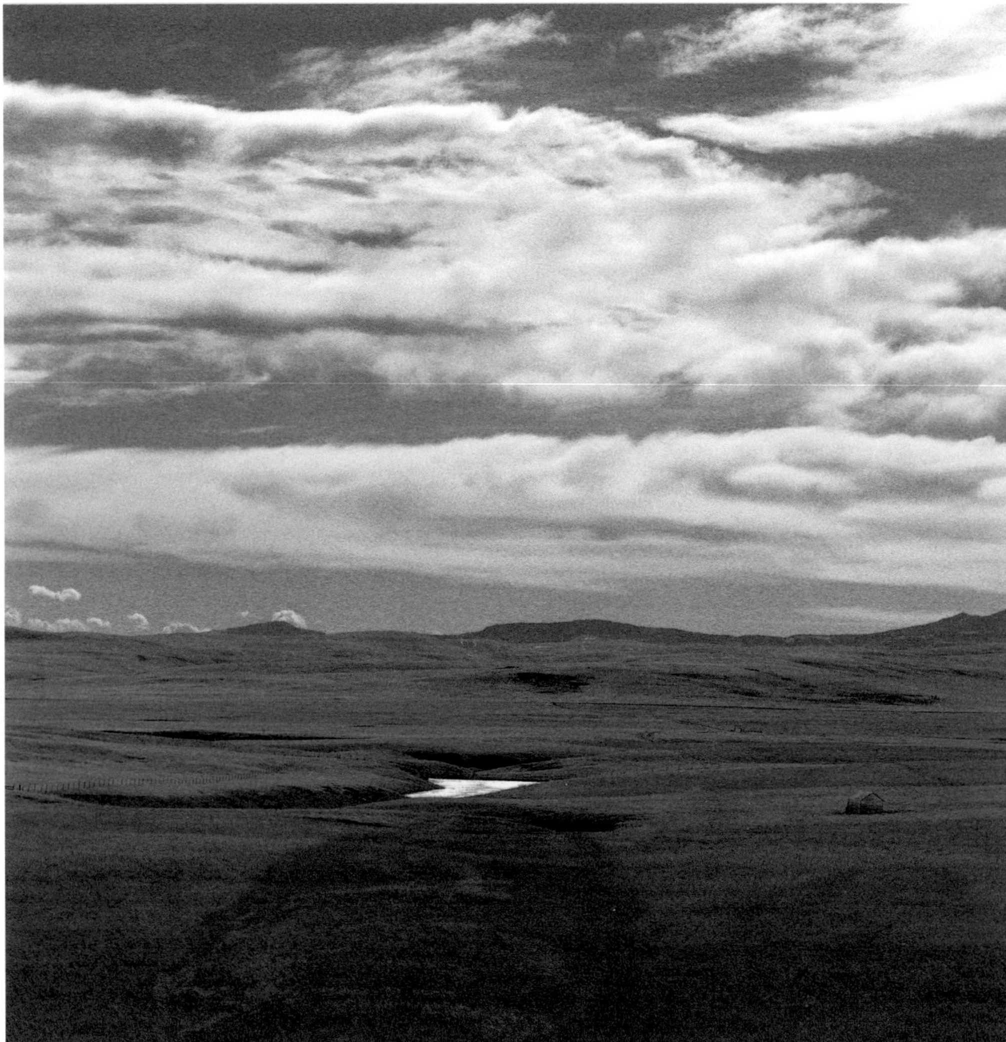

Spring Walk

Small weeds bouncing in the wind,
tearing at the pavement.
Mid-morning, the street empty.
Dust on someone's window,
their unwatered plants.
And here, the earth packed, the dandelion's
leaves notched, prostrate; cold.
How broken down the world is,
ancient, in the April light.

May

The first clear day after weeks of cloud:
like smoke, the pollen drifting from the firs.

Sex

What are you, bright thread
that nothings us,
on which we're strung? — the blaze
inside the husk, and what
the husk is for:

burnt, cast off, clamouring with joy
to be a thing that dies.

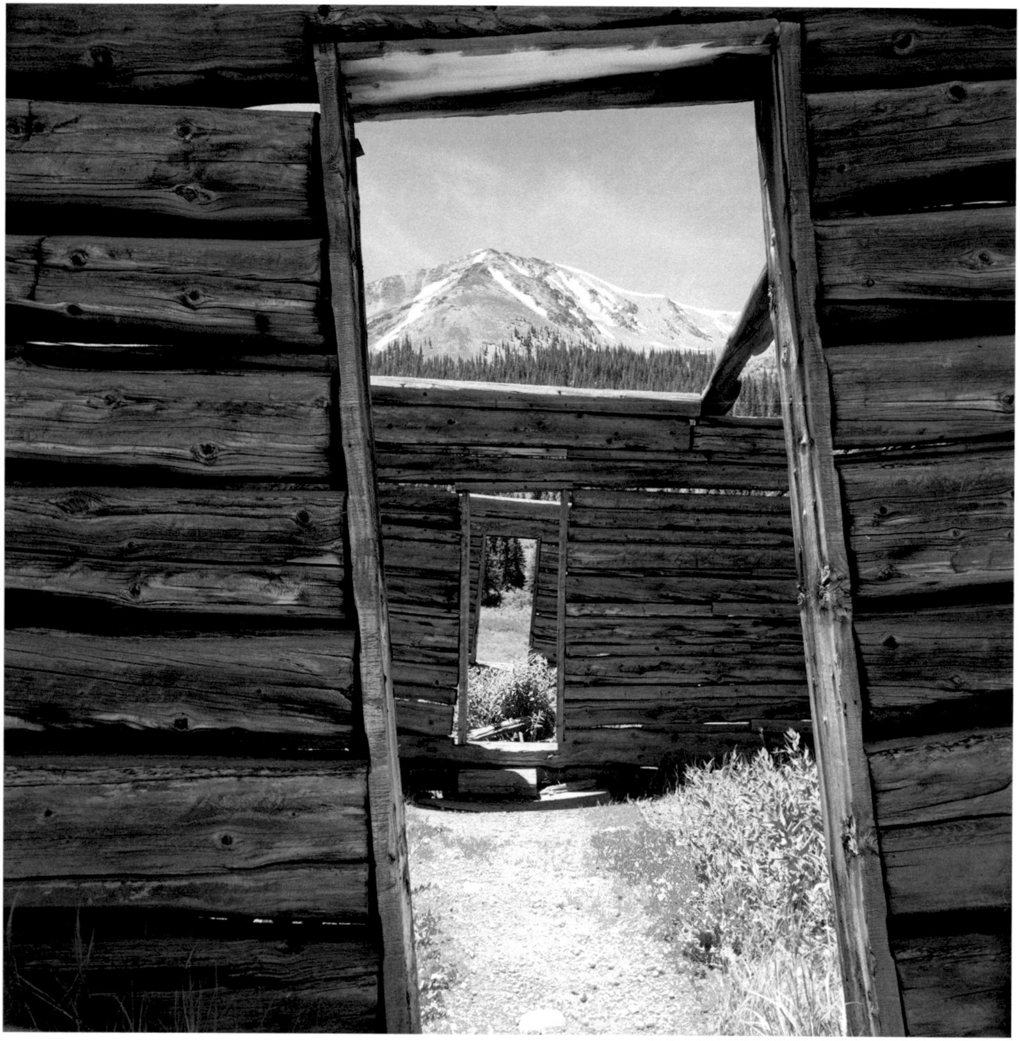

Spring in the Mountains

On the first day in June,
the wind's mouth
is full of glinting teeth.
But its sorrow is
it has no hands.
It sings *tether tether —*
                    and we,
who do not understand
the language of the wind,
hear only *Soon you too,*
let go, let go.

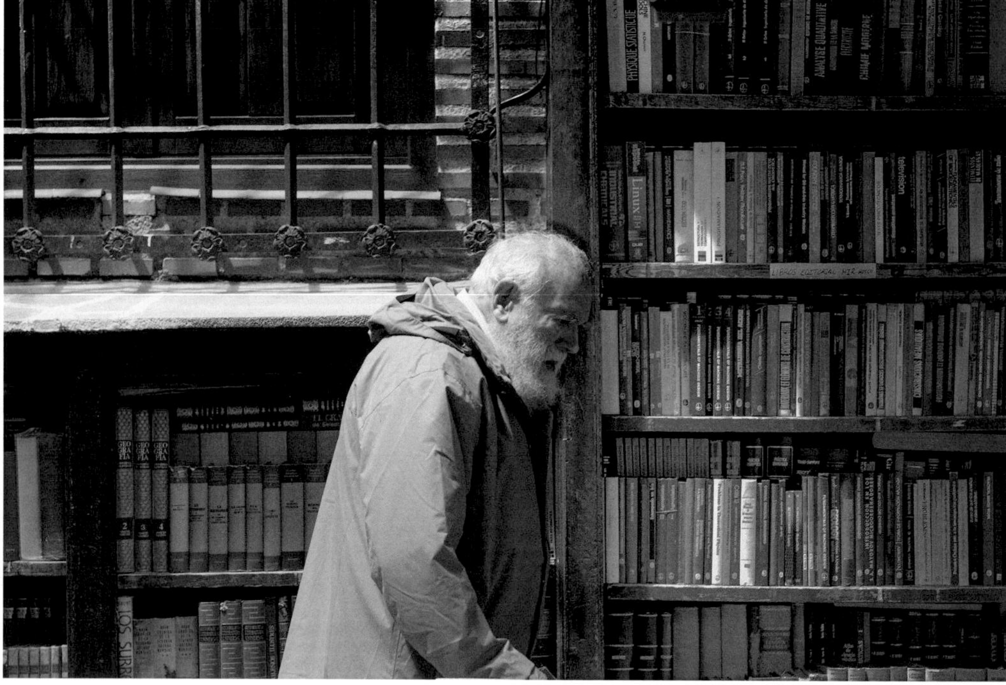

Old Books

The world is once again a desert.
But head out anyway
among the banded cliffs,
the untalkative sands.
There's a place you know. A seep,
the water sweet, miraculously
cool. No more than a trickle,
and the tin cup pocked and battered.
But it has never, down all the centuries,
run dry.

Old Blues

I wish I knew why we don't get along.
The visions that you've sprung in me —
Jiménez, Szymborska, Pindar, Plath … I could name
a hundred more. Not music, no, but
still I've had to change my life.
The hubbub and the laughter there
behind the golden windows of your house.
And yet I'm out here, cold, boot-stupid,
in the dark and rain. Language,
why don't I love you more?

The Great Composers

Where do they learn such sorrow?
It must be the body, its imponderable
separateness. The hydrothermal vents
where it began: did they weep, too,
those first molecules of methanol
and formic acid? Was it the darkness,
or the light?

At the Jewish Memorial in Prague

The walls of names, the articulate smoke
of them. My body, a dog
standing in the muddy road to Terezin,
staring after.

                    You came, then,
and we went out of there, my body
pressed against yours,
going only where you were going,
without words.

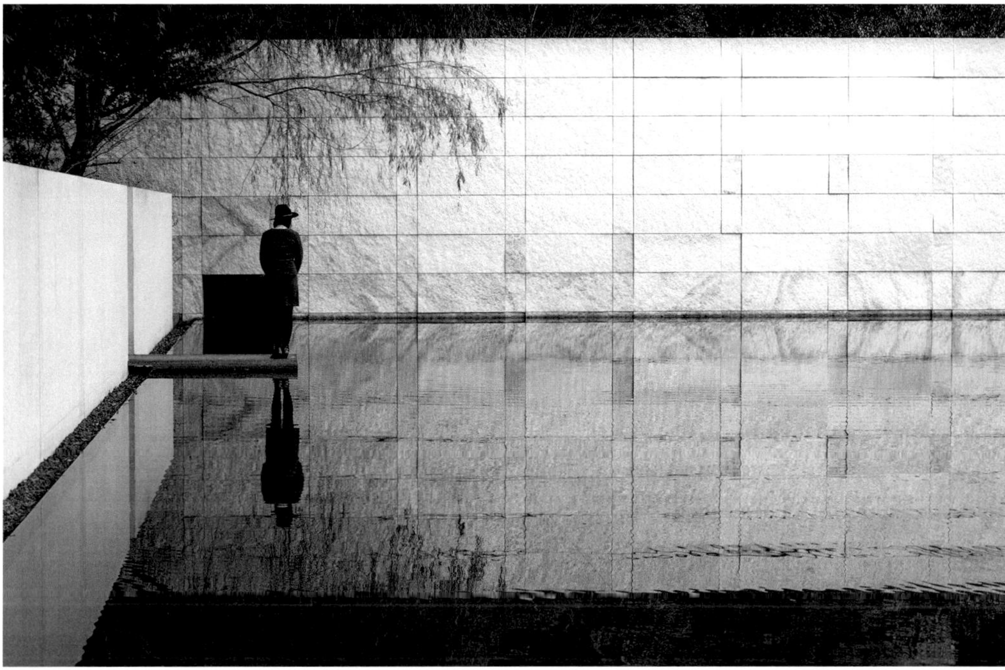

Standing in line at the bank after reading lines by Roo Borson

Today's art, even yesterday's — how much
of it matters anymore?
But your words, old friend.
The tears down my old face.

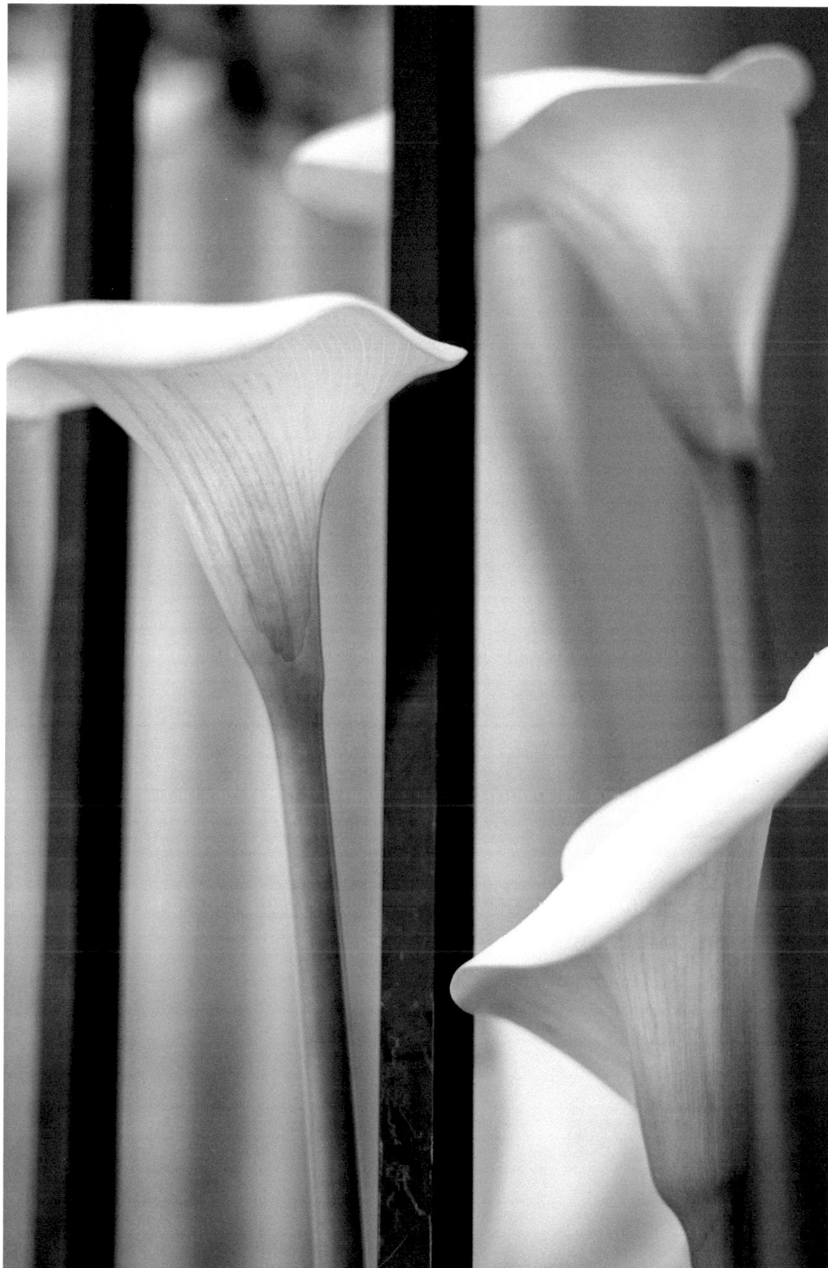

After Flight

How beautiful the evening is, here
on the earth: here,
in the bronze shadow of the mountain,
the cascade of cedar, and the huckleberry
bent with fruit. But you are still dreaming
of the life that you saw, that was yours,
there, on the curved bed of the sea,
the flat-bottomed clouds passing above.

Night Air

As if the bones were porcelain, those
on which you climb down to the bottom
of the well, the water both of us must drink,

and when sleep reassembles us,
as if the skin were polished, too,
and without sound, from nowhere,

night air slips across it
frictionless, the life that joins us with the world
again translucent and unbreakable.

Sunshine

The weight of it, the way it gives way
as you walk into the field.
The stillness that it loves: the slough sedge,
black heads hung like jewels,
the sleeping newt, the voiceless stone. As though
the weight that glows inside each thing
were happiness. All of us,
heaped, gold, sunken
at the bottom of the sky.

Light Industrial Park

The frontier's quiet at the end of the day,
machines abandoned to the slanting sun,
their noise gone elsewhere, highways in the distance.
The empty cabs of the forklifts, open to the weather,
the parallel lines the light makes
skimming the stacked pipes.
Someone in overalls heading home,
the clank of the latch as the gate falls to.
The rattle of a price tag lifting in the wind.

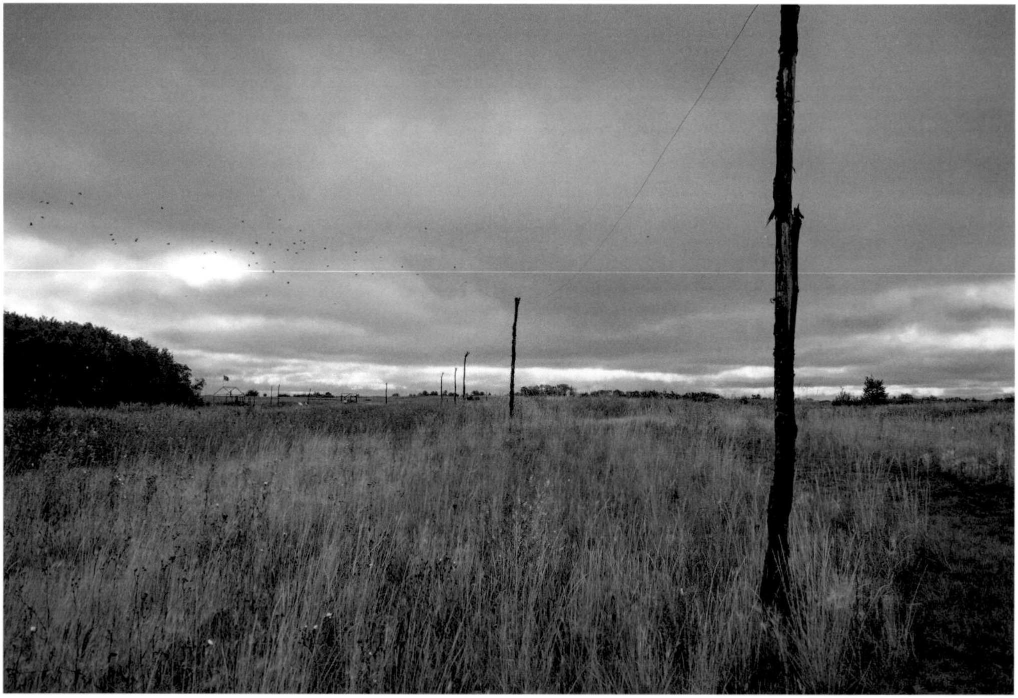

Befriending Wind

Ah, wind, you're too extreme for me.
How could I greet you as yourself
        but naked on the prairie?
How could I invite you in
        except I tear the curtains from the windows,
        loose these pages to the sky with all their
        words, words, words, words, words?

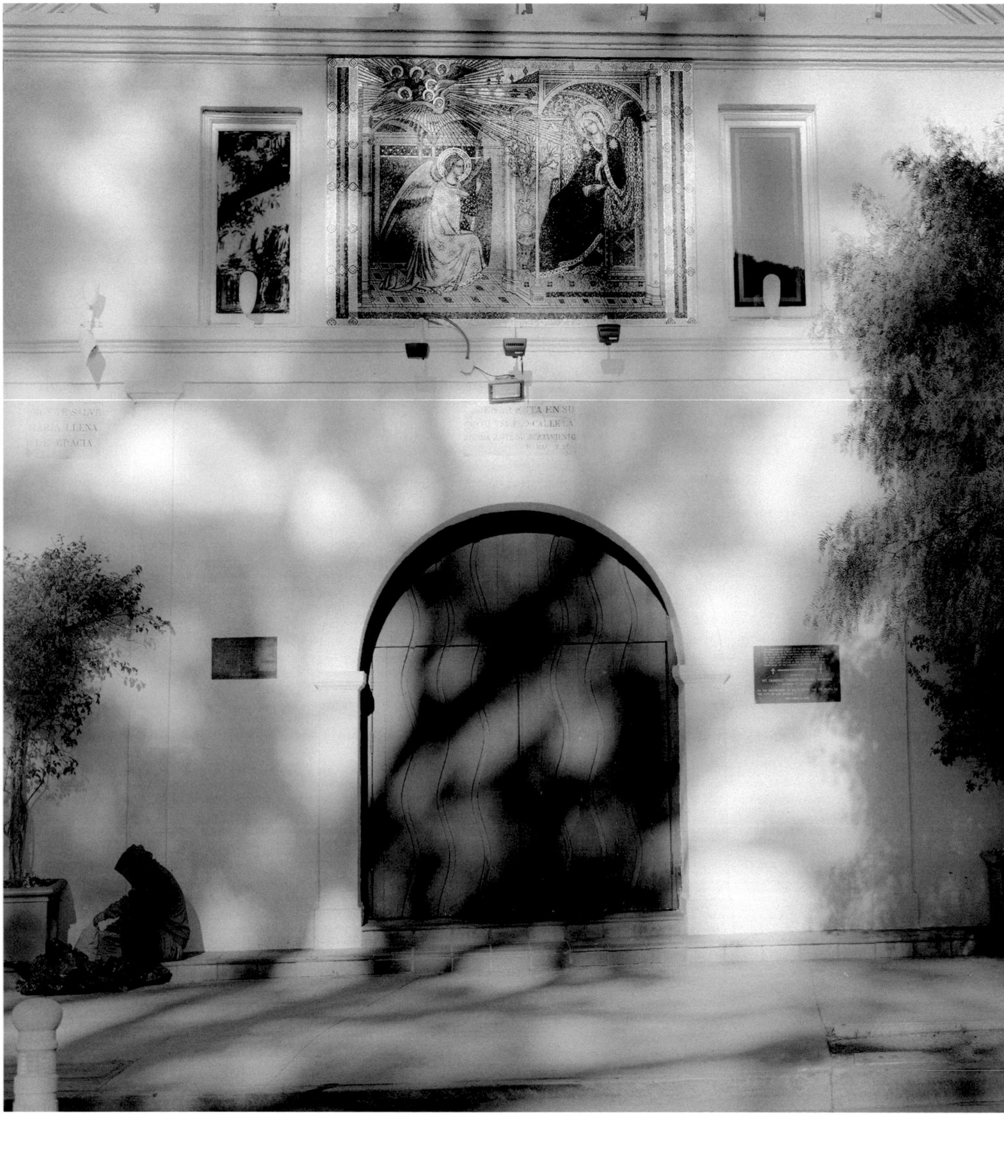

Crying

The wind comes down
the long slope of the mountains,
comes in from the foothills, thrashing its tail.
People run inside, they bolt their doors,
cats hunker under bushes, and the bushes
hold on tight. Everything
moves back into its place,
stops. Closes its mouth. Sits down.

Later, the moon will rise,
over the clean streets, the polished stones.
High in the bell tower,
a few dry leaves. And the bells,
motionless.

Late Style

The problems are insoluble.
Work all your life, you won't
come close. Might as well say
what you think. What you thought

all along, trying to please
those ghosts, the keepers
of keys, the mathematicians
counting on their fingers in the dark.

Drought

Sun rising red through smoke.
In the dream I wake from,
outside the winter house where cold
meant minus forty with a wind,
I bend to pull the broken stem
up through the snow, and the snow
— the snow — is weightless, dry,
a kind of powdered styrofoam,
warm to the touch. The land
now covered in it. Oxygen
withdrawing from the air.

Feet

Which is worse, the body
or the mind? Pressing, always straining
to be somewhere else:
the headlong weight of them.
But the feet

are kind, they hope
we're trying. "No," they say,
just, "no" — and only after hours
of bad posture and
stomping around.

It's to themselves
that they repeat the lesson
once we've gone to sleep:
the instep's petalled curve,
the artless bones.

Lullaby

Don't let grief frighten you.
Standing outside, in the mind,
its silhouette is winged and cavernous.
But what brought you here: is past.
No need to lock the door.

Don't let grief frighten you.
Bring it in to sit down by the fire.
In the hearthlight, you will see its face
is human, its hands
are empty like your own.

Lavender

A scent with the blue of mountains in it
and the peace of solitary shade on hot afternoons.
I love you as the bees do, one by one,
the others lost now, their companionable hum.
That Christmas, still a child, I took the bus alone,
right downtown, to sink my arms up to their elbows
in the huge box at the Hudson's Bay.
The distances behind us. The distances ahead.

String Quartet

What was it that you heard
half a century ago, transfixed there
at the top of the stairs, the evening
pink above suburban rooftops, the radio
left playing by the homework
on your desk? How did you know,
you who knew nothing
of Europe, or deafness, or love,
that someone finally was telling the truth?

Badlands

Moonrise. The end of the world.
Who has known such happiness?

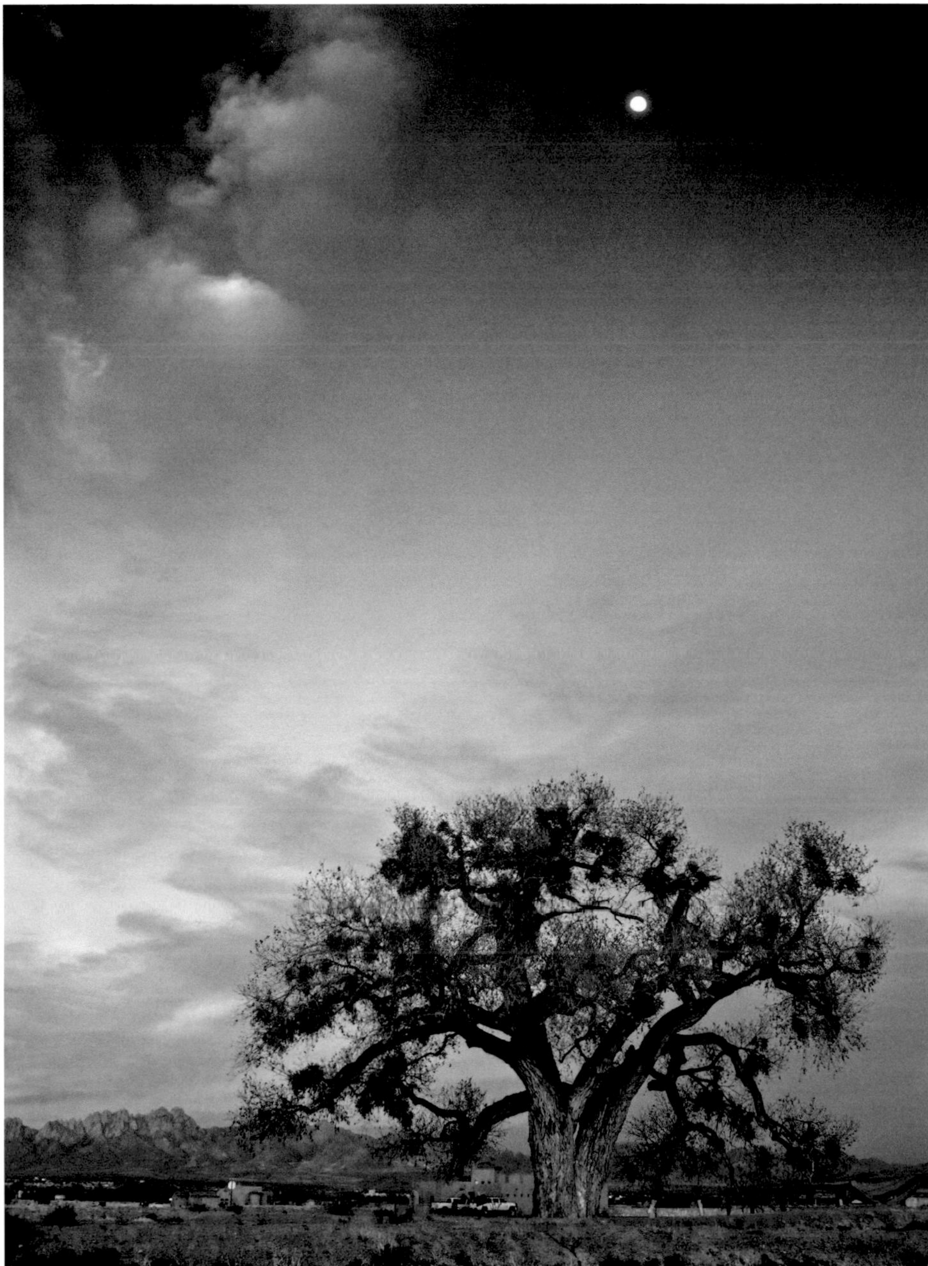

Rocky Shore

Sharp sun and a big northwest wind,
the world a breathless rumpus
underneath. Gulls up,
wheeling high against the light, tide
running fast out in the strait.
Earth with its arms wide open:
uncountable its loves.
Even you. Even me.

Harvest

I understand despair. History,
after all. But my griefs are simple.
No great dream or longing that I've learned
won't be fulfilled.

A thought arises from the dark earth
of the body — we don't know how.
Uncountable the days the shining seed
drifts in the wind and disappears.

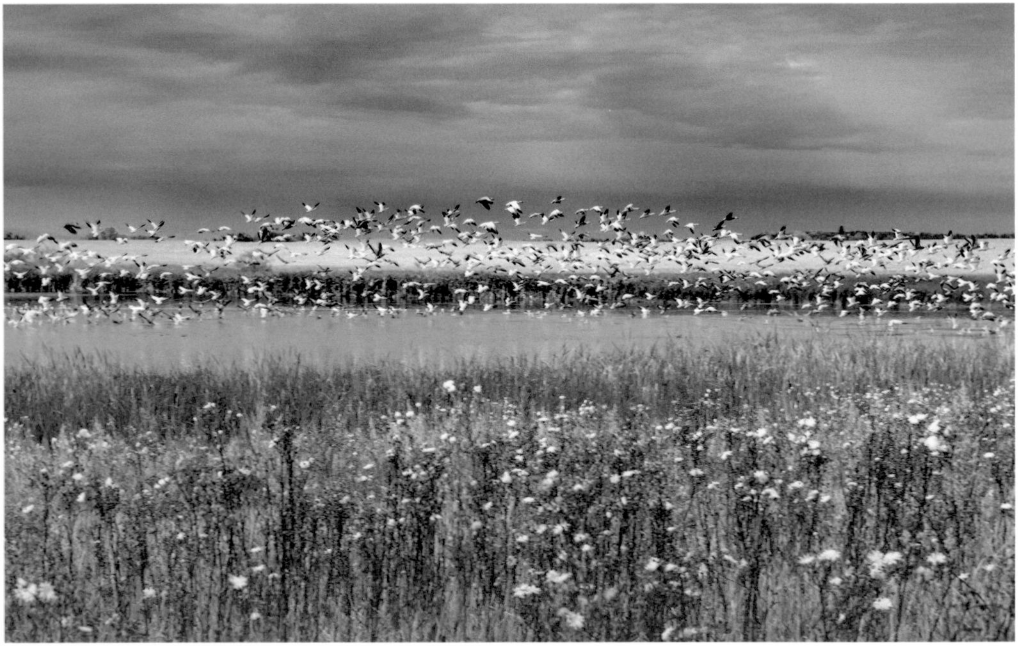

Earth Season

The day after rain dawns clear:
high summer's sudden end.
Every leaf glossy, opaque, the sky
preoccupied, intent. Distance
even in the corn, the celery —
who are you, human? They race away
into themselves, listening only
to a foreign wind.
Grief sharper than frost,
this abandonment of ecstasy.

Ars Poetica

Disappearing into silence, refusing to use words,
it's no way to make a name.

The heron arches its great wings,
without a sound takes flight.

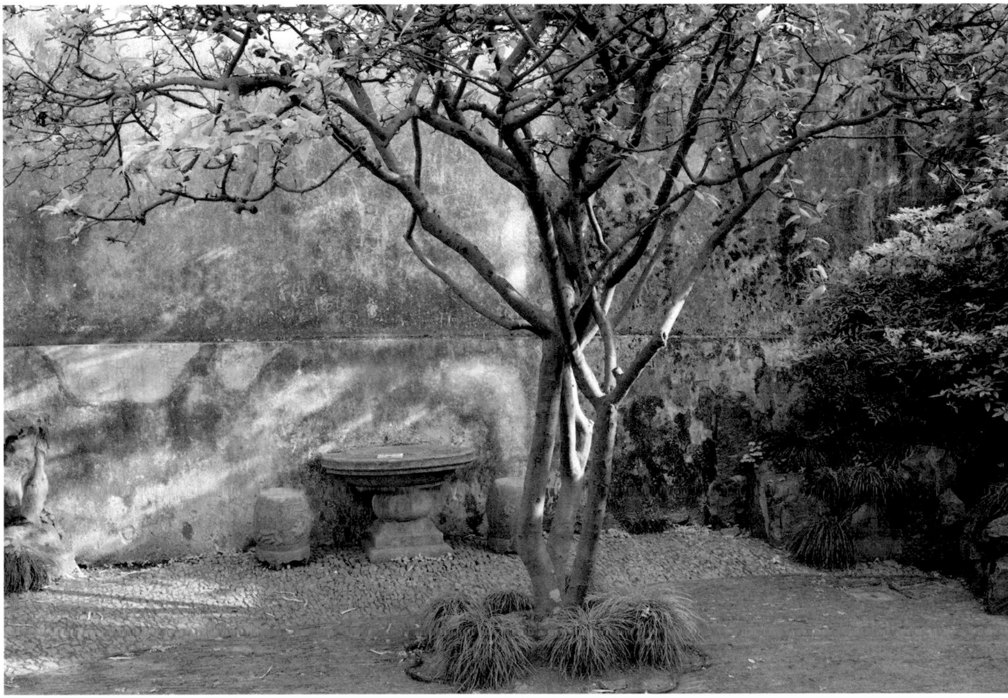

Autumn

Dusk gathering, no lights on,
the rain that's falling
drop by drop down from the eaves.

Footsteps passing, then a car.
The leafless world

on which the rain is falling
drop by drop
by drop.

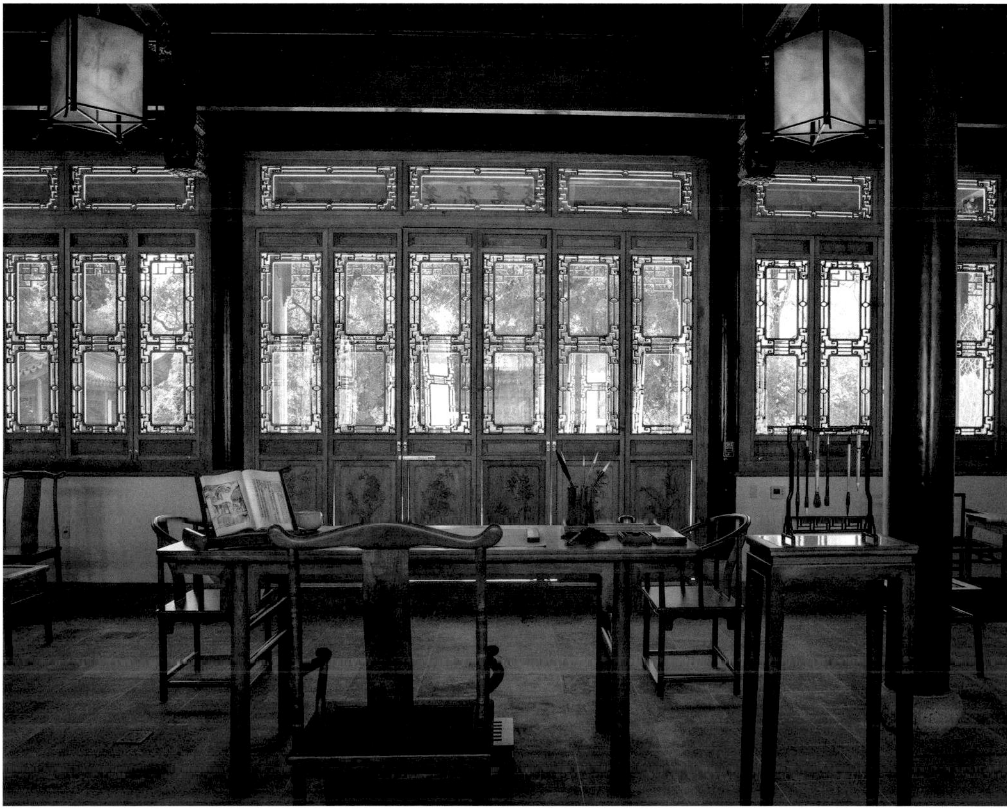

Translation

Struggling with the lexicon, the grammar crib,
straining towards sense, suddenly
across twenty centuries, out of
unimaginable foreignness, some other mind
leaps up to meet your own.
As though your heart and his were eyes, and
above the smoke, the hordes, the shouting,
those eyes locked.

View from the Ferry

Last car on the upper deck
so as we pull into dock I'm standing
aft in the open air.
The ferry stalls, slow as the sun
this time of year. 3:00 p.m.,
already dusk gnaws at the edges
of the shadows. We drift
toward rush hour, eyes front.

And there — behind a tangle
of guy ropes, pilings, warning signs —
a mixed flock of fifty, maybe more,
buffleheads, scoters, mergansers,
dipping, swivelling. It rides
the swell as one mind,
weightless
in the gusting light.

Up at four a.m.

Not night, not morning: dead light,
the breath in you gone cold,
your third eye opening on everything
unloved. But your terror
shows you do not understand.
The housework of the universe
is done. Or not. An ember in the stovebox
faintly glows. Or not.

Waking

Sleep, what pulls us from you? You
who walk the dark cellular corridors of the body
in your dusk-blue robes. Old, and twenty thousand times
I've woken, but can't remember how it's done.
Some border crossed, but borderless,
some turning, but the path to it erased.

Each day you've stood at the end of the final hallway,
the rim of the world gone white. The hook of sunlight
lifts us, gasping, to a new transparency. And we twist
with our sudden weight, the spangled brilliance of it —
the sluice of dreams prismatic, flashing,
as it drops away.

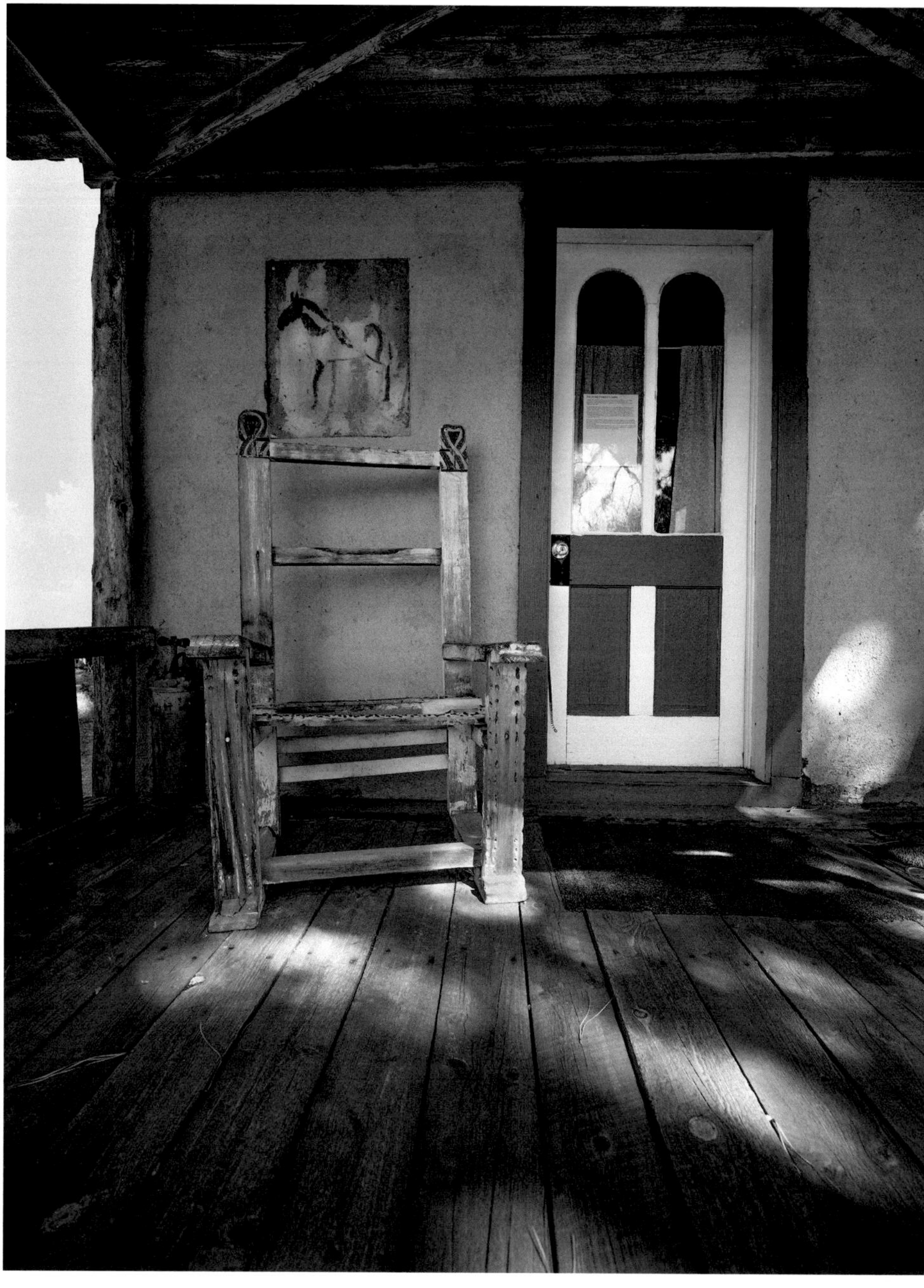

Winter

Feet bare on the bare boards
of the porch. No moon.
What was it you once asked me?
The dead fruit, sweet, in its glass jars.

Acknowledgements

Our very warm thanks to everyone at Freehand Books, especially Kelsey Attard, Natalie Olsen, and Glenn Rollans, for their keen interest in the project, and for their responsiveness, generosity, and flexibility in the face of its unusual demands. We would also like to extend special thanks to Robert Bringhurst for his superb design sense and his alacritous attention to detail.

An earlier version of this book was published as a limited edition in 2020 by Barbarian Press under the title *Fifty-six Ontological Studies*. We are grateful to Jan Elsted, Crispin Elsted, and Apollonia Elsted for bringing that project to fruition, and for their kind permission to pursue a trade edition.

A number of poems in this volume also appeared prior to the Barbarian Press edition, some in different forms. Jan Zwicky offers sincere thanks to the editors of the following publications: *Arc*, *CV2*, *Dusie*, *Eighteen Bridges*, *The Fiddlehead*, *The Malahat Review*, *The Society*, and *Vallum*. She also thanks Roo Borson for her excellent eye and ear, and Robert Bringhurst, Darren Bifford, and Warren Heiti for their insightful readings.

Robert Moody would like to thank Wendy McKay-Moody for her consistent encouragement in his pursuit of photography, her invaluable technical help, and her keen sense of style.

The venture has been not only an invigorating challenge, but a source of delight and inspiration. Our final thanks, each to the other.

PHOTOGRAPH LOCATIONS

12 *Table, Chair, Bed* · Dorothy Brett Cabin, D. H. Lawrence Ranch, New Mexico

17 *Strait of Juan de Fuca* · Muir Creek, British Columbia

20 *Clearing Storm* · Macaulay Point, British Columbia

25 *Driftwood* · Dungeness Spit, Washington

29 *Sakura* · Chitose, Hokkaido

31 *Lightfall* · Walt Disney Concert Hall, Los Angeles

32 *Ice Lake* · Porcupine Hills, Alberta

36 *Independence* · Independence Pass, Colorado

38 *Bookseller* · Madrid

43 *Water Mirror Garden* · D. T. Suzuki Museum, Kanazawa

45 *Calla Lilies* · Oak Bay, British Columbia

50 *Dominion Telegraph* · Old Humboldt, Saskatchewan

52 *Our Lady Queen of Angels* · La Placita, Los Angeles

61 *Cottonwood* · Mesilla, New Mexico

64 *Snow Geese* · East of Humboldt, Saskatchewan

67 *Lingering Garden* (Liu Yuan) · Suzhou, Jiangsu Province

69 *Scholar's Study* · The Huntington, San Marino, California

74 *Chair* · Homesteader's Cabin, D. H. Lawrence Ranch, New Mexico

Sixty-Seven Ontological Studies was designed, assembled, and set in type by Robert Bringhurst on Quadra Island, British Columbia. It was printed by Hemlock Printers in Vancouver. The paper is Spicers' Pacesetter Silk, an FSC recycled sheet. The text face is Brioso, designed by Robert Slimbach and released by Adobe Systems, San Jose, California, in 2003. The titling face is Diotima, designed by Gudrun Zapf von Hesse and cut in metal at the Stempel Foundry, Frankfurt, in 1953.